101 AMAZING DAD SKILLS

FIRST PUBLISHED IN THE UNITED KINGDOM
IN 2017 BY

PORTICO
43 GREAT ORMOND STREET
LONDON
WCIN 3HZ

AN IMPRINT OF PAVILION BOOKS COMPANY LTD

ISBN 9781911042815

A CIP CATALOGUE RECORD FOR THIS BOOK IS
AVAILABLE FROM THE BRITISH LIBRARY.

10 9 8 7 6 5 4 3 2 1

PRINTED AND BOUND BY CPI GROUP (UK) LTD CHATHAM

DESIGNED AND ILLUSTRATED BY BECKY BRICE

EMBARRASSING DAD JOKES COURTESY OF IAN ALLEN

THIS BOOK CAN BE ORDERED DIRECT FROM THE
PUBLISHER AT WWW.PAVILIONBOOKS.COM

101 AMAZING DAD SKILLS

PORTICO

Hats off to all those that do the job of mum and dad on their own, but this book is dedicated to you dad — with love.

1. MAKE ROAST CHICKEN FIT FOR A KING
(or a prince at least)

This is a recipe adapted from Tom Parker Bowles' excellent book *Let's Eat*, handed down to him by his mother, Camilla, who just happens to be married to Prince Charles. It is a super-easy low-maintenance staple roast chicken recipe, and may very well become your No.1 Sunday favourite.

Pre-heat the oven to 220·C / 425·F / Gas 7. Take your chicken and rub salt and pepper all over and in the cavity (Roast Chicken 101 — take out the giblets!). Then rub the skin with butter or, if you are feeling adventurous, work your fingers under the skin near the breast and thighs and push butter in there. Turn the bird over and smother the underside in butter too. Next, take a lemon and pierce it a few times, then stuff it in the cavity. Place in a roasting tin, and wash your hands.

Roast in the oven for 20 minutes, then turn the oven down to 180°C / 350°F / Gas 4. Set your timer for 25 minutes per 500g, or in old money 23 minutes per pound. The bird is ready to come out when you pierce it with a skewer and the juice is no longer pink (or see skill 44). Rest for at least 15 minutes (the chicken, not you) before serving.

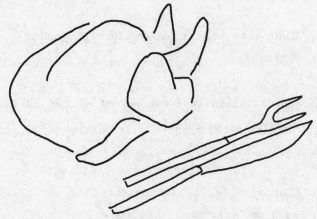

Enlist as many accomplices as possible, and begin the run-up to serving the meal while doing your best impression of Gordon Ramsay commanding a Michelin-starred kitchen. Tie a tea towel around your head and see what swear words you can get away with — or apply your own bleeps.

Once the meal is served, relax in the knowledge that the head chef never does the washing-up.

2. 10 EMBARRASSING DAD JOKES WHILE SHOPPING

1. What shop sells right-angled triangles?
   Pythag R Us.

2. I once pushed in front of one of the Seven Dwarves in a queue... he wasn't happy.

3. Dad: I wish I'd brought the piano with me.
   Kid: We're in the supermarket. Why do you wish you'd brought the piano?
   Dad: Because I've left the shopping list on it.

4. Customer: I'd like a Comet pasty, please.
   Butcher: Don't you mean a Cornish pastie?
   Customer: No, a Comet pasty is a little meatier.

5. Customer: I'd like a book by Dickens, please.
    Shop assistant: Certainly, sir, which one?
    Customer: Charles.

6. I went to a self-service supermarket last
    night with my zebra... it cost me £254 to
    get him out.

7. Two lions were in a supermarket. One said
    to the other, 'It's quiet in here today...'

8. Customer: I'd like a comb please.
    Assistant: Yes, sir, do you want a steel one?
    Customer: No, I'll pay for it.

9. Customer: How much are your melons?
    Grocer: This one is a pound, and you can
    buy a second one for 50p.
    Customer: I'll just have the second one then.

10. Customer: Do you have any OXO cubes?
    Assistant: No, we're out of stock.

3. MAKE A PIÑATA

By now you may have spent a significant amount of time at parties that your kids have been invited to, and I am hazarding a guess that at some point you have witnessed the ritual of the unbreakable piñata. It usnally ends in a frenzied Game of Thrones-style battle involving hordes of pillaging kids smashing, jumping and tearing at the piñata. This can be fun to watch in other people's houses, but the collateral damage to property can be high, so for your own kids' party here is an easy solution that hits the sweet spot between impenetrable and flimsy submission.

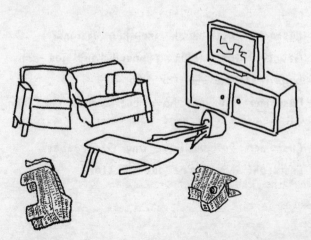

1) Find a vacuum cleaner dust bag. They vary in shape and size depending on the type of vacuum cleaner they are for, but generally they are made of thick paper and have a reinforced hole with a membrane attached that secures the hose/nozzle into the bag.

2) Assess the shape of the bag and look for a natural fit in terms of crafting it into a recognisable figure, character or animal.

3) Before you start crafting, push your sweets and mini toys into the hole covered by the membrane. It's best to use sweets and chocolate that have a wrapper, and toys that don't break easily. If the bag is now full and holds its shape then good — if not then insert a balloon into the space and inflate.

4) Next, get sticky. Gather together crepe paper, kitchen-roll tubes and other bits and bobs you will be using to create your masterpiece. Using glue, do your best to fashion something recognisable, and if it ends up looking like a vacuum cleaner bag with coloured tissue stuck on it, then c'est la vie. The kids will be more concerned with what's inside it.

5) Finally, leave to dry and then attach to a washing line, end of a broomstick or a crystal chandelier (not).

| 4. | ## GET

COMPOSTING

'You smell that? Do you smell that? Compost, son. Nothing else in the world smells like that. I love the smell of compost in the morning.'

If Alan Titchmarsh had been cast in *Apocalypse Now* rather than Robert Duvall it might have been a very different movie, but there is something strangely alluring about the odour of compost. Composting could become one of those weird obsessions that you should probably keep to yourself, but as it can cut down on your kitchen waste by up to 30 per cent AND provide you with free fertiliser for life, then go on, knock yourself out.

1) Get yourself a composting bin — the black dustbin-sized ones with a little shovel-sized door at the bottom are good.

2) Position it on a well-drained site where any excess moisture within can escape, and also where your new best friends, worms, can make their way in.

3) Start composting. Good — grass cuttings, coffee grounds, fruit and veg peel, crushed egg shells, weeds, leaves, tea bags/leaves, paper and cardboard. Bad — meat, cooked food, dairy products.

4) To turn or not to turn, that is the question? If you leave it as is, you will have a nice mulch within three months, but if you want to get down and dirty then find a good fork and give it a thorough mix every week. Turners suggest that this creates compost quicker.

5. ROADTRIP PLAYLIST

'Get your Ford Focus running / Head out on the M25 / Looking for a campsite / And a Welcome Break on the way'

Steppenwolf didn't sing those song lyrics in their iconic 1968 classic 'Born to Be Wild', but when the road comes a-calling it's time to plan a roadtrip playlist. This is an almost unique opportunity to try and imprint your immaculate musical taste on a captive audience, but don't lay it on too thick or your kids might become traumatised and always equate long, boring motorway journeys with your idiosyncratic musical taste. You don't want them to turn to the dark side and put their earphones in.

So — mix it up a bit and try and bring them with you, both figuratively and literally.

Side A	Side B
- 'Born to Be Wild' — Steppenwolf	- 'Ace of Spades' — Motorhead
- 'Pull up to the Bumper' — Grace Jones	• 'Fools Gold' — Stone Roses
• 'Paranoid Android' — Radiohead	- 'I Drove All Night' — Roy Orbison
- 'Drive My Car' — The Beatles	• 'The Distance' — Cake
- 'Song 2' — Blur	- 'Driving in My Car' — Madness
• Four Seasons: 'Spring' — Vivaldi (Nigel Kennedy)	• 'Autobahn' — Kraftwerk

6. KEEP THE SHOWER ROOM CLEAN

Perhaps not the most amazing Dad skill there is, and certainly not the most exciting, but this simple tip could save you time and money, while also cutting down on the cleaning chemicals that we wash into the drains every day.

For roughly the same cost as two bottles of bathroom cleaner, it is now possible to buy a small squeegee and a microfibre cloth. If you can, buy a squeegee that also has a sucker attachment to enable it to be stuck somewhere convenient and always at hand the moment you emerge gleaming from your ablutions.

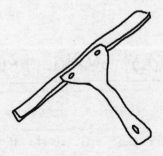

Simply switch off the shower, grab the squeegee and do your thing on the tiles and glass, making sure to overlap on each stroke. Then grab the dry microfibre cloth and polish off the leftover drops. You should have sparklingly clean surfaces that you can see your face in.

Finally, incentivise and enlist any junior eco-warriors in the house by demonstrating that a little elbow grease and some well-chosen tools can replace harmful cleaning chemicals.

7. VERY SMALL BRIBES

1) Find somewhere that still stocks those old-fashioned tins of travel sweets, and purchase one. Barley sugar is best.

2) Pocket the tin and carry it around with you, doing your best to ignore the annoying clanking sounds.

3) Not to be overused, but when you really need to, pop open the tin and bribe the kids to do what you want.

4) Never speak of this.

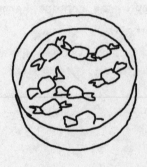

8. PRESS WILD FLOWERS

As much about the act of gathering them as the processing into decorative delights, this is a lovely way to pass a morning.

1) Go on the hunt for wild flowers — so that means in the woods, countryside and scrubland. Not somewhere that looks cultivated (e.g. your local park's flowerbeds) or privately owned. Only pick where you see a multitude of the same flower and taking a few won't jeopardise the population.

2) Get the flowers home and as quickly as possible place them between a folded sheet of newspaper, and then between the pages of the largest, heaviest book you can find. A world atlas would do the job.

3) Pile some other books on top and leave for around a week until all the moisture has gone.

9. BEACHTIME FUN

FOSSIL HUNTING

It is a well-known fact that without small children and their Dads throwing stones into the sea there would be no waves. There is something hypnotic about the waves and the satisfying plop as a thrown pebble hits the water. Another absorbing pastime is the act of smashing rocks in pursuit of fossils.

To begin the hunt you will need some goggles, a small geological hammer (the one with a square end on one side and a wedge shape on the other) and an idea of what sedimentary rock looks like (it has layers).

The best time to look for fossils is in the winter, as the seams of sedimentary rock are more likely to have come away from the cliffs or been exposed. For obvious reasons do not hammer at the cliff face or climb it. If you are lucky enough to find a fossil then it is most likely to be an ammonite.

If you can't find any sedimentary rock then don't worry — simply spend some time smashing up rocks for the hell of it. You may have to give up the hammer at some point to let your kids have a go.

10. MAKE BUTTERBEER

All Harry Potter fans will at some point persuade you to make Butterbeer, the favourite tipple of the regulars at the Three Broomsticks. Below is an approximation of what you might find at the various Warner Bros. Harry Potter theme parks.

1) Take a beer tankard and fill with American Cream Soda.

2) Dollop a scoop of butterscotch ice cream on top (or vanilla if you can't find that).

3) Allow the bubbles to turn the ice cream to foam, and then serve, encouraging all to cultivate a foam moustache.

11. MAKING SENSE
OF IT ALL...

'Men should always change diapers. It's a
very rewarding experience. It's mentally
cleansing. It's like washing dishes, but
imagine if the dishes were your kids, so
you really love the dishes.'

CHRIS MARTIN

12. MAKE A DEN WITH SHEETS

'What a spiffing idea!' exclaimed Tarquin, his cheeks crammed full of Uncle Bertie's delicious home-pressed ox tongue.

This does seem like a skill from a different time, but kids are never happier than either industriously creating their den, or then reclining among its splendour. All you need to do to set them up is:

1) Either indoors or outdoors, find suitable places to tie string, and then, using sheets and clothes pegs, put up a canopy.

2) The rest is up to them. Chances are they will find every soft toy, soft furnishing, soft fruit (basically anything soft) and chuck it in the den.

3) You may be required to serve drinks and snacks.

13. MAKE SURE YOU HAVE GOT EVERYTHING

- ☐ Tent
- ☐ First-aid kit
- ☐ Sun cream
- ☐ Alcohol hand gel
- ☐ Headache pills
- ☐ Extra batteries
- ☐ Toilet roll
- ☐ Kitchen roll
- ☐ 5-litre bottle of water
- ☐ Camping stove
- ☐ Pots/pans
- ☐ Plates/cups/bowls
- ☐ Kettle
- ☐ Cooking utensils
- ☐ Cool-bag
- ☐ Ketchup and condiments

- ☐ Washing-up bowl
- ☐ Tin opener
- ☐ Bottle opener
- ☐ Old newspaper
- ☐ Firelighter
- ☐ Matches/lighter
- ☐ Head-torch/torch
- ☐ Camping chairs
- ☐ Bin bags
- ☐ Duct tape
- ☐ Spare tent pegs
- ☐ Mallet
- ☐ Sleeping bags
- ☐ Pillows
- ☐ Extra duvets
- ☐ Special blankets

14. DAD DANCING WORKSHOP

Perfect your moves and
embarrass your kin to boot!

THE POGO

As everyone else flees from the dance floor,
this is your cue to make like it's 1976. With
the able assistance of a few like-minded Dads
it is time to show your kids what PUNK was
all about. Decide on whether to channel Sid
Vicious, Johnny Rotten or Joe Strummer,
and pull the relevant snarl. As you bounce
spasmodically on the dance floor try to make
contact in a sweaty embrace with your fellow
pogoers in mid-flight. Spitting is optional but
not advised at weddings.

15.

SING A
CAMPFIRE SONG

This traditional song is sung to the tune of 'London's Burning' and is a great way to start the singing off for the evening. If you are feeling adventurous then try this in 'the round', where the second half of the group begins the first line as the first half of the group commences the third line. Also, this song contains what may be the greatest word in the English language — 'gloaming'.

Campfire's burning, campfire's burning,
Draw nearer, draw nearer,
In the gloaming, in the gloaming,
Come sing and be merry.

16. ROAST CHICKEN EPISODE 2 — THE GRAVY STRIKES BACK

A roast chicken isn't fully dressed until it is bathed in delicious gravy. See skill 1 for how to roast a chicken.

1) While the meat is resting on a plate, tilt the roasting tin and spoon off any excess fat — leave a little in the tin for good measure.

2) Then put the tin on a high heat and add a glass of dry white wine. Boil off the alcohol, then add about 450ml (1 pint) of chicken stock and reduce, mashing in a few bits of any veg you may have ready, at the very least a couple of roast potatoes (see skill 23). The veg should help thicken the gravy while adding flavour.

3) Once you are happy with the seasoning, sieve into a suitable jug and keep warm.

17. TELL A SCARY STORY

Gathered in the gloaming around the campfire, toasting marshmallows on sticks — time for a scary story...

Announce that you have a scary story to tell, hint it might not be suitable for all the kids present to hear, and let them persuade you to go ahead nevertheless. Wait for complete silence and, in your best Long John Silver voice, begin...

'TWAS A DARK AND STORMY NIGHT, AND THE CAPTAIN SAID, GATHER ROUND ME, LADS, AND I'LL TELL YOU A TALE, AND THIS IS THE TALE THAT HE TOLD...'

Let the tension build and go on...

'TWAS A DARK AND STORMY NIGHT, AND THE
CAPTAIN SAID, GATHER ROUND ME, LADS, AND
I'LL TELL YOU A TALE, AND THIS IS THE TALE
THAT HE TOLD...'

Some of the audience will begin to cotton on
— once more...

'TWAS A DARK AND STORMY NIGHT, AND THE
CAPTAIN SAID, GATHER ROUND ME, LADS, AND
I'LL TELL YOU A TALE, AND THIS IS THE TALE
THAT HE TOLD...'

By this stage you will be pelted with
marshmallows and you may need to make a
hasty exit. Obviously this skit is to be
repeated every single time you go camping
until you hang up your head-torch for the last
time... Only to be rolled out again when your
grandchildren arrive!

18. NIGHT-TIME PARK RUN

You are having one of those days where you haven't even got out of your pyjamas yet and somehow it is already getting dark outside, and everyone is getting a bit narky with each other. Could it be time to play the 'Night-time park run' card? This can only be played a maximum of once a month, and the rule is that everyone in the house must participate.

Once the 'card' has been played everyone has five minutes to assemble at the front door ready to go. Hot-foot it to the park and run until everyone is exhausted, or the light has gone.

Return home with a slight sense of achievement for the day, and everyone in a slightly more chipper frame of mind.

19. RECITE A POEM

Useful to be able to pull out of the kit bag around the campfire, commit this little pearl of genius to memory and put on your best Stephen Fry impression to deliver it.

JABBERWOCKY
Lewis Carroll

Twas brillig, and the slithy toves
    Did gyre and gimble in the wabe:
All mimsy were the borogoves,
    And the mome raths outgrabe.
'Beware the Jabberwock, my son!
    The jaws that bite, the claws that catch!
Beware the Jubjub bird, and shun
    The frumious Bandersnatch!'
He took his vorpal sword in hand:
    Long time the manxome foe he sought —
So rested he by the Tumtum tree,
    And stood awhile in thought.
And, as in uffish thought he stood,
    The Jabberwock, with eyes of flame,
Came whiffling through the tulgey wood,
    And burbled as it came!
One, two! One, two! And through and through
    The vorpal blade went snicker-snack!
He left it dead, and with its head
    He went galumphing back.
'And, hast thou slain the Jabberwock?
    Come to my arms, my beamish boy!
O frabjous day! Callooh! Callay!'
    He chortled in his joy.
Twas brillig, and the slithy toves
    Did gyre and gimble in the wabe;
All mimsy were the borogoves,
    And the mome raths outgrabe.

20. CLEANING INSIDE WINDOWS

Impossible not to execute this task without at some point subconsciously humming the tune to the George Formby classic 'When I'm Cleaning Windows', and if that thought wasn't already imbedded somewhere in your brain then it sure as hell is now!

That's Formby, not Foreman

Making light work of this chore is almost entirely dependent on the investment you make in equipping yourself with the best tools for the job. You will need a sponge, a squeegee, a bucket and a lint-free cloth such as a microfibre cloth. In addition you will need some kind of cleaning solution. Many people swear by warm water with a squeeze of washing-up liquid, while others use a mixture of one part white vinegar to one part water.

Douse the sponge in the cleaning solution, squeeze out any excess, and then get scrubbing. Follow quickly with the squeegee, in a side-to-side motion overlapping each stroke, and then finally wipe away any excess fluid with the lint-free cloth.

21. DEPLOY THE PROBLEM SANDWICH

'Sam is coming over for dinner
tomorrow night...

which means you will have to
tidy your room now...

but you can choose what you
have for dessert tomorrow?'

22. MAKE A NATURE TRAIL

Arrive suitably early at the site of the planned expedition — local woods, beach, country walk. Plan a circular route that will lead you back to your starting point and choose a duration that will suit everyone's attention span.

Using natural materials to hand that won't be blown away, arrange arrows that point in the right direction at key points on the trail. Try to disguise these signifiers slightly to provide a bit of jeopardy. To add an extra dimension to the trail plant a few riddles to be solved scrawled on paper that might reveal a snack or treat hidden among some of the natural surroundings.

For example:

From this marker take 10 steps back,

Reversing your way back down the track.

And to your left, down by your boots,

Find hidden treats among the roots.

23. MAKE 'THE BEST ROAST POTATOES IN THE WORLD'

Not many people know this*, but according to the now-departed restaurant critic and film director, Michael Winner, Sir Michael Caine makes the best roast potatoes in the world. Along with his love of chill-out or trance music from the 90s, these nuggets of trivia were revealed in his 2009 appearance on the BBC Radio 4 classic show Desert Island Discs. What follows is an approximation of Sir Michael's instructions on the best way to make roast potatoes.

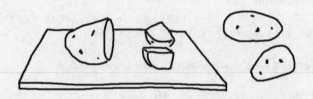

Sir Michael doesn't suggest a particular potato variety, but a general 'white' all-purpose (Maris Piper or King Edward) should do the job. He recommends peeling them and boiling the potatoes until soft at least on the outside.

Then:

'get them absolutely dry, let them steam and go dry, put the lid back on and shake 'em till they go all fluffy and then put them in cold olive oil with rosemary and sage in it'.

Pop them in the oven for an hour or so at a medium-high heat and job's a good 'un.

*Not many people know that Sir Michael never really used this phrase, and only referenced it as an in-joke in the 1983 movie *Educating Rita* and then later for a trivia book with all profits going to charity.

24. 10 EMBARRASSING DAD JOKES FOR ON A PLANE

1. Captain: Right, I'm afraid the plane's going down, is there anyone here who can pray?
   Flying officer: I can.
   Captain: Good, start praying, we're one parachute short.

2. What did the idiot say when the plane went through turbulence?
   'Oh no, an earthquake!'

3. What do you get if you cross an airport runway with a herd of cows?
   A herd of dead cows.

4. Traveller: I'd like a return flight, please.
   Airline clerk: Certainly, sir, where to?
   Traveller: Back here, you fool!

5. What did the Red Baron say when he bailed out during World War One?
'Bi-plane!'

6. What did the cat say when he hijacked the plane?
'Take me to the Canaries.'

7. Nervous flier: It's my first time in a plane, you will bring me down safely, won't you?
Pilot: I've never left anyone up there yet.

8. Teacher: You were supposed to draw a picture from the Bible — what's that aeroplane doing there?
Pupil: It's the Flight to Egypt, and that's Pontius the Pilot.

9. Why did the man wake up in the morning to find a plane outside his bedroom?
He'd left the landing light on.

10. Customer: A pint of bitter and a packet of helicopter crisps.
Barman: I'm sorry, we've only got plane crisps.

25. STAGE A GRUESOME PARTY GAME

Good for Halloween parties, and birthdays too, this uber-traditional game really gets the party going. Each partygoer must take a turn to put their hand into 'Beelzebub's Boxes' and feel the gruesome contents. Are they brave enough?

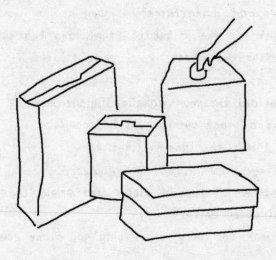

1) You will need to have stockpiled and decorated enough boxes (shoe/cereal etc.) for each bravery test, and you will need to cut a small hole in each to enable touching without spying what is in the box.

2) For each box choose as many as you like from the following: cooked spaghetti (worms), peeled grapes (eyes), dried apricots (witches' ears), soft toy (dead rat), pistachio shells (finger nails) and turd-shaped gingerbread (dog poo).

After everyone has had a go, award prizes for correctly guessing what was in each box.

26. DESTROY WEEDS

Weeds can become another magnificent obsession, like maintaining a perfect lawn, or stacking the dishwasher. Don't let this chore get out of control, and take appropriate action. You've tried those nasty chemicals, you've tried gardening by moonlight, and you've even considered Astroturf. Time to blitz them.

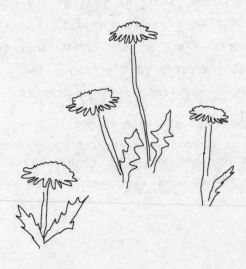

1) A weed wand is like an oversized Bunsen burner that you attach a small camping gas cylinder to. It is designed to be used to eradicate unwanted growth on concrete patios and paths. Get one.

2) Fire up the weed wand and blast the weed, taking care not to set your house on fire at the same time.

3) The heat will cause the weed to shrivel up and die over the next few days — it should not come back.

It's not the most eco-friendly way to get rid of weeds as what you save on not putting more chemicals into the water table you lose on contributing to the greenhouse effect, but it's certainly the most fun!

27. HOMEWORK
PLAYLIST

Despite your best efforts it is the evening before
the deadline for that homework task that absolutely,
definitely, wasn't going to be left until the last
minute. You make a mental note to be stricter, to
diary and calendar every significant date of your
significant minor's educational schedule.

And then you remember how you were back in the
day. Maybe, like you back then, they will argue
that they perform better under the pressure of a
looming deadline?

No matter — now is not the time for reflection,
it is time for action. You can help get those brain
cogs turning with a bespoke inspirational playlist.
Or use this pre-prepared mix:

Side A	Side B
• 'The Big Ship' — Brian Eno	• 'The Staunton Lick' — Lemon Jelly
• 'The Lark Ascending' — Vaughan Williams / Nigel Kennedy	• 'Blue in Green' — Miles Davis
• 'Little Fluffy Clouds' — The Orb	• 'No Surprises' — Radiohead
• 'Sinnerman' — Nina Simone	• Symphony No. 3 OP. 36: 'Lento e Largo' — Gorecki
• 'The Great Gig in the Sky' — Pink Floyd	• 'Pale Blue Eyes' — The Velvet Underground
• 'Desafinado' — Joao Gilberto	• 'Gymnopedie No. 1' — Érik Satie

28. A LIGHT HOUSE CLEAN*

Like most things in life there is always more you can do to improve your surroundings, and if you are lucky enough to have got through family life so far without ever having to roll up your sleeves and get cleaning, then it is likely to be at someone's expense, either yours fiscally or theirs time-wise.

If you don't have the luxury of a cleaner, and if you aren't already well versed in the art of cleaning, then now is the time to start getting down and dirty. It's common sense really, but starting at the top of the house, or one end of the property, start to sweep through, grabbing as much as you can from the floors and surfaces that are quick fixes to put away. Crucially do not start flicking through a book or magazine you've picked up and then find you have forgotten what you were doing — keep your focus.

Next, back to the beginning with dusters, polish and feather duster in hand. Once again you want a metronomic rhythm as you waltz serenely from room to room, dusting as you go. Utilise the feather duster for any cobwebs in the corners and skirting boards, and the polish for surfaces. Do not use polish on the TV, mirrors, computer screens or any kind of glass (see skill $\boxed{49}$ for how to tackle this challenge).

And then it's back to the top of the house again, this time equipped with the vacuum cleaner (see skill $\boxed{41}$). If you have one of those cordless ones then you will have a built-in timer before the battery and your patience for the task run out. With or without a cordless, once again keep the pace up — better to have cleaned badly then never to have cleaned at all.

Finally, attack any non-carpeted floors with a mop and bucket, and leave the kitchen and bathroom for another day. Done.

* NB, not to be confused with a lighthouse clean, which requires a lot more time and a very long ladder.

29. MAKE PAPIER-MÂCHÉ

The basis of many crafty projects, this is a simple and versatile material that makes a huge amount of mess — so your kids will love it!

1) In a large bowl mix some white PVA glue with half the amount of water until it is smooth.

2) Tear up a newspaper into strips and then soak a strip in the glue mix, removing any excess solution as you go.

3) The best base for your project is generally a blown-up balloon (easily popped), but you can use any shape. Just bear in mind that you will in most cases need to leave an exit to extract the mould from the finished artwork.

4) Lay the strips over the mould one by one, and alternate layers horizontally and vertically three times. Scrunch up the paper to make any features, and then layer strips over these to smooth it over.

5) Leave to dry for around 24 hours, which is about the same amount of time it will take you to clean up afterwards.

30. LIVING WITH INSTAGRAM 📷

Instagram is supposedly for teenagers over 13 years old (with a parent's consent) but it is a well-trodden path to gain access from as young as 10 years old without anyone's permission. This is something you may not always be able to influence in the short term, but can certainly influence in the long term (confiscation of the device in question should do the job).

If you have granted your permission, or are letting them get on with it, then you will have already considered the well-documented negative aspects of social media applications. In an ideal world Instagram should be a place where your children can learn about polite, concise communication through text and images. It may foster an interest in photography and make them think about the language of imagery. It may also spawn an interest in social media marketing, which may become a career choice. As I said — in an ideal world!

31. BEACHTIME FUN

GET YOURSELF BURIED
IN SAND OR PEBBLES

The great thing about this is that your kids will almost definitely see the burying as the best part of this deal and, although you will feign indifference, we all know that this is a perfect opportunity to grab a cheeky nap. Two things to consider: Firstly, if this is a pebbly beach then it is advised to make sure your hands are covering your family jewels — those stones can be quite heavy. Secondly, if it is your plan to take a nap, don't forget the sunblock.

32. CAST THE SPELL
OF SOPOR

When it's the night before Christmas, a
birthday, or a 4a.m. departure to the
airport, and they just can't seem to get to
sleep — then it is time to cast the Spell
of Sopor. Get them back into bed and,
lying on their back with their eyes closed,
begin the spell.

SOMNUS, SOPOR, DORMIO, NOX
TENSE YOUR TOES, AND THEN RELAX
SOMNUS, SOPOR, DORMIO, SNOOZE
TENSE YOUR CALVES, THEN LET THEM LOOSE

SOMNUS, SOPOR, DORMIO, NOX
TENSE YOUR KNEES, AND THEN RELAX
SOMNUS, SOPOR, DORMIO, SNOOZE
TENSE YOUR THIGHS, THEN LET THEM LOOSE

SOMNUS, SOPOR, DORMIO, NOX
TENSE YOUR BUM, AND THEN RELAX
SOMNUS, SOPOR, DORMIO, SNOOZE
TENSE YOUR WAIST, THEN LET IT LOOSE

SOMNUS, SOPOR, DORMIO, NOX
TENSE YOUR TUM, AND THEN RELAX
SOMNUS, SOPOR, DORMIO, SNOOZE
TENSE YOUR CHEST, THEN LET IT LOOSE

SOMNUS, SOPOR, DORMIO, NOX
TENSE YOUR HANDS, AND THEN RELAX
SOMNUS, SOPOR, DORMIO, SNOOZE
TENSE YOUR ARMS, THEN LET THEM LOOSE

SOMNUS, SOPOR, DORMIO, NOX
TENSE YOUR NECK, AND THEN RELAX
SOMNUS, SOPOR, DORMIO, SNOOZE
TENSE YOUR CHEEKS, THEN LET THEM LOOSE

By now they might be asleep — if not, just
leave the room as calmly and with as little
conversation as possible.

33. MAKE LEMONADE

If the grocer gives you un-waxed, organic, ethically sourced lemons — make lemonade!

As a refreshing, healthy pick-me-up on a hot day or as an entrepreneurial venture to raise money at the school fair, this is one of those skills that can be pulled out of the hat at a minute's notice to keep bored minds busy. Also, once the knife work is done you can leave them to it.

1) Locate the bullet blender from wherever it has been gathering dust for the past year or two, 2–3 un-waxed lemons and the white caster sugar.

2) Chop one of the lemons and, taking out the seeds, put it in the blender, along with the juice of the rest of the lemons. Add about 3 tablespoons of the sugar and the same again of water, and blitz until you have a puree.

3) Finally, add water a glass at a time and whizz until you reach the sweet and sour spot. You might need to add a little more sugar (best to oversee this bit).

34. DAD DANCING WORKSHOP

Perfect your moves and embarrass your kin to boot!

NORTHERN SOUL

Strap on your braces, cock your trilby and set your legs to oblivion. Your aim is to secure a circle of clapping spectators, ideally not all laughing at you, as you take centre stage. Once you have your audience, begin to tell the ancient story of man vs dance floor. As the track approaches its end it is time to really get the crowd's attention, show them that there is life in the old dog yet.

It is the moment to attempt, for one last time, the ultimate Dad dance move... the splits. You should be warmed up, you should be lithe, you should be feeling the spirit of the Wigan Casino running through your veins. Now is the moment. Time stands still, the crowd gasps, you stretch your legs, and, and ... your trousers split and you put your back out.

35. CRACK A COCONUT

Whether you have dragged your kids to the local summer fair, or they have dragged you, then you may find yourself in possession of a 'loverly bunch of coconuts' that you have finally won after embarrassingly too many goes on the coconut shy. To harvest your bounty (pun intended):

1) Using a clean screwdriver and a hammer carefully poke a hole in at least two of the eyes.

2) Place the coconut on top of a glass and tilt to drain to the water.

3) Wrap the coconut in a tea towel and, ideally on a concrete surface, tap until you hear cracking.

4) Using the hammer, nurture the crack and split the coconut into as few pieces as possible.

5) Now chisel the white flesh away from the husk using the screwdriver, and hopefully it will come away cleanly in one glorious piece. This is where the knack is.

36. MAKING SENSE OF IT ALL...

'It was my father who taught me to value myself. He told me that I was uncommonly beautiful and that I was the most precious thing in his life.'

DAWN FRENCH

37. EASY LOVE IT OR HATE IT MIDWEEK PASTA

This is a super-quick store-cupboard dinner
for when you have a thirty-minute window
to feed everybody before your pick-up or
drop-off adventures continue. It's a variation
of Nigella Lawson's recipe, which she cites as
originating from the Queen of Italian cookery,
Anna Del Conte. As you may have guessed, the
'love it or hate it' reference has something
to do with Marmite, and for all who didn't
guess then insert the word Vegemite. If you
are still struggling then Marmite is a
yeast-based extract traditionally spread on
toast, and was more recently advertised with
the slogan 'Love it or Hate it'.

According to Anna Del Conte the water in
which you cook pasta should be as salty as
the Mediterranean. Use any pasta you like, and
when cooked drain off the water, keeping
back a cup of the salty water should you
want a bit more moisture for the sauce. Then
add 2 teaspoons of butter to 1 teaspoon of
Marmite, stir and repeat until you love it.
Serve with grated parmesan and chopped
tomatoes.

38. KNOW WHAT A GOOGLY IN CRICKET IS

Cricketers can spend a lifetime trying to master the art of the googly, so if you can teach your child to get anywhere near this goal they will be most likely to make it into any team they try out for.

In a nutshell, the googly is a delivery that looks like a leg break (a ball that spins away from a right-handed batter's legs to the off side), but actually bounces and spins towards the batter's legs.

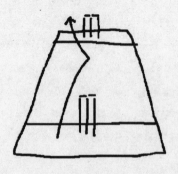

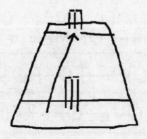

The trick of the bowler is to lull the batter into a false sense of security, consistently spinning the ball away from the batter's legs, and then drop in the googly which, unless detected, spins into the legs and ideally between the bat and the leg pads and on to the stumps.

To bowl a googly you need to make the ball spin clockwise out of the hand rather than anticlockwise as in regular leg-spin, all without the batter 'picking' it and adjusting their shot accordingly. This is a top skill in cricket, and if your child seems interested in taking up this challenge then it might become a lifelong obsession, which could lead them to international sporting glory (or just to the local rec).

39. RECOMMENDED BOOKS TO FOSTER A LOVE OF READING

'There's more to life than books, you know. But not much more,' sang Morrissey in the Smiths song 'Handsome Devil'. You may very well agree, as you hold this book in your hand. But if you can get your children thinking of books as entertainment, rather than something they use at school, then you may help fuel a fire that will burn not just in their academic years but all through their life.

The best children's books can be read to your children and/or by your children. I'm sure that together you will have your own ideas on what they want to read, but here are a few series options anyway.

1) Roald Dahl. The Shakespeare of children's authors, consistently relevant and deliciously dark — *Fantastic Mr Fox* is a good place to start.

2) *Mr Gum* by Andy Stanton. Totally hilarious (for everybody) tales of the revolting Mr Gum and his idiotic friends. Excellent audio CDs performed by the author are available too.

3) *Tom Gates* by Liz Pichon. Super-accessible and highly illustrated tale of regular school/family life.

4) David Walliams. Following in the grand tradition of Roald Dahl and featuring everyday children in extraordinary circumstances.

5) *A Series of Unfortunate Events* by Lemony Snicket. Given a new lifeline by the excellent Netflix series of the same name, Snicket creates a Dickensian tale of triumph in the face of adversity.

6) *Harry Potter* by J.K. Rowling. Astoundingly successful series and a core text for any child approaching the tumultuous teens.

[40.] DESCALE A KETTLE

This is another one of those jobs no one wants to do that somehow falls under your remit. This method is very easy and doesn't use any environmentally damaging chemicals or cost more than the price of a lemon. It also provides an opportunity to prank the fellow kettle users of the household if you 'accidentally' forget to warn them of your actions — it could leave a sour taste in their mouth!

1) Chop a lemon, or two if you have a large kettle.

2) Put the lemon pieces along with any juice into the kettle and fill to the maximum line.

3) Squish the lemon in the water with a spoon for a bit, and then bring to the boil, twice.

4) Leave overnight for the natural acids to do their magic, and you should find that a gentle scrub will remove any remaining limescale.

41. CHOOSE A GOOD VACUUM CLEANER

A note on vacuum cleaners — there is a reason that most domestic and industrial cleaning professionals choose a Numatic Henry cleaner. They are incredibly hardy, relatively inexpensive and provide better-than-average performance. And they have a smiley face on the front!

42. THE SCHOOL RUN

The <u>FIRST</u> rule of the school run
is don't forget to pick up.

The <u>SECOND</u> rule of the school
run is don't forget to pick up.

43. <u>10 EMBARRASSING DAD JOKES AT THE DENTIST</u>

1. Did you hear about the dentist who became a brain surgeon?
His drill slipped.

2. Dentist: That's the biggest cavity I've ever seen... biggest cavity I've ever seen.
Patient: There's no need to repeat yourself.
Dentist: I didn't, that was an echo!

3. Dentist: I've got some good news and bad news. The good news is your teeth are all fine.
Patient: What's the bad news?
Dentist: All your gums have got to come out.

4. Has your tooth stopped hurting yet?
I don't know, the dentist kept it.

5. I hear you had all your teeth taken out?
I did, yes, and I'll tell you what, never again!

6. Patient: How long will it take to do the filling?
    Dentist: About ten minutes.
    Patient: You charge an awful lot for ten minutes.
    Dentist: I can make it last an hour if you want me to.

7. Patient: Since you fitted these false teeth I can't pronounce my f's and th's properly.
    Dentist: Well, you can't say fairer than that then.

8. Patient: I love this new chair you've got — it's great the way it goes in and out instead of up and down.
    Dentist: Will you please get out of my filing cabinet!

9. What are a dentist's favourite two letters?
    DK.

10. What does the Dentist of the Year receive?
    A little plaque.

44. SERVE PROPERLY COOKED MEAT AT A BARBECUE

It is surprising how many of us will temporarily commit to a vegetarian diet at the first whiff of a barbecuing sausage. We have all been handed a slightly damp bread roll containing a charcoal-encrusted morsel with a startlingly pink centre, and then reluctantly taken a bite as the host looks on. The aftermath endured a few hours later is enough to ensure that we will never repeat the mistake again.

Luckily technology has stepped in once again and solved this perennial problem. For the cost of a couple of glasses of wine you can now equip yourself with a digital thermometer that will take the guesswork out of whether your meat is safe to eat or not.

Simply follow the guide temperatures and all will be well. Remember that these temperatures are just a minimum guideline and you may enjoy meat cooked well done; this is just the minimum temperature at which meat is safe to consume. Don't forget to leave the meat to rest.

Some meats are suitable to eat rare, so if you like your steak bloody then just ensure that any exterior surface of the meat is cooked to the minimum guideline temperature.

The following is reproduced from the US Department of Agriculture guidelines, but use your common sense if it doesn't look right.

BEEF, PORK, VEAL & LAMB
Steaks, chops, roasts
145F (62.8C) and allow to rest for at least 3 minutes.

GROUND MEATS
Beef burgers, sausages, meatballs etc.
160F (71.1C)

ALL POULTRY
Breasts, whole bird, legs, thighs, and wings, ground, minced poultry, and stuffing
165F (73.9C)

FISH AND SHELLFISH
145F (62.8C)

45. <u>MANAGE A</u> <u>SLEEPOVER PARTY</u>

Eventually you will have to give in and agree to this, but remember to use it as a bargaining chip for at least six months in advance of the event.

1) Plan a physical event of some kind before dinner. Swimming, a park visit or a two-hour high-intensity interval training session... something to really tire them out.

2) Then back home for a meal which pretty much has to be a pizza delivery. Don't forget to chop and arrange some vegetables in a vain attempt to add something healthy to the meal.

3) After dinner, time to get them active again. Motivate the kids to help make: a) a smoothie b) a milkshake c) popcorn or finally, if you are feeling brave, then d) a freakshake (see skill 58).

4) While you are tidying the kitchen the kids will need to get into their PJs, and arrange their sleeping bags in the allocated room that has been sacrificed for the evening.

5) Time to get into position. All snacks and drinks should be contained within a designated serving zone, and all personnel should be zipped up in a sleeping bag. Commence movie number one, which should be of a relatively light tone conducive to light banter and horseplay.

6) As the film comes to an end it's time to take the pulse of the party. Is everyone comfortable? Maybe a goodnight text or call home to calm any nerves?

7) Now you know everyone is in for the long haul, it's time to make THE DEAL. In return for a final treat of a hot chocolate (WITH MARSHMALLOWS!) all parties must agree to a final lights-out at an agreed time.

8) Then serve the hot chocolate and leave them to it. At the designated lights-out time, tuck them in and say good night. Hard-liners will wait outside the door until silence falls — they may have a long wait...

9) Next day see skills 64 and 80 for breakfast ideas and hope parents arrive promptly at the designated pick-up time.

10) Once you are home alone with your super-tired kid tread carefully. Even the hint of a request to help clear up will be met with a full-scale meltdown. You have been warned.

46. WASH YOUR BIRDFEEDERS

'Wash your birdfeeders? Why would I want to do that when I could be lying in the hammock playing Angry Birds?' you ask. Insert your own shaming punchline here.

Not many people know this but if you don't wash your birdfeeders regularly then they are prone to promoting infectious and potentially fatal diseases. So while you are happily re-filling your feeding devices assuming that you are contributing to improving the local wild bird population, you may well be hindering its progress.

This is one of those lonely Dad skills that will go unrewarded and unheralded by your family, but a Dad's gotta do what a Dad's gotta do.

1) Take down all the feeders, empty out any uneaten feed and scrape off any droppings and general gubbins.

2) Using a screwdriver where necessary, dismantle the feeder as best you can and submerge and scrub in a bucket of warm soapy water. A strong disinfectant odour may deter birds, so just use a mild detergent; a brush and plenty of elbow grease will do the job.

3) Leave until thoroughly dry (otherwise the new feed might go mouldy), and then re-hang the feeders in a new location. If you don't relocate every 4—6 weeks then the droppings and feed that gather underneath may also become a health hazard for the birds.

47. TEACH THEM TO SWIM (OR GET SOMEONE ELSE TO)

This may well be one of life's lessons that we leave to the professionals rather than teach ourselves. The expense of lessons can be counterbalanced by the idea of relaxing by the pool with the sun beating down as you watch your children cavorting in the water, safe in the knowledge that they are perfectly capable of swimming themselves out of danger. And you don't have to blow up the water wings any more.

48. <u>GET HYGGE</u>
<u>WITH IT</u>

The definition of hygge seems to be a bit of a grey area, but loosely it seems to refer to some kind of shared everyday cosiness. In terms of parenting this should be right up there as a core skill, but it seems that we are only just learning about it from our Scandinavian friends.

However, in the spirit of openness, plan a surprise hygge afternoon. Pick a wet wintry day and, on returning to the house after a brief outing, serve hot chocolate or tea, with toasted teacakes, crumpets etc., and sit around the fire (if you have one). Play games, wear big jumpers and grow a beard for the occasion (assuming you are able).

49. CLEAN YOUR COMPUTER AND TV SCREENS

If you are a geeky Dad then you will be uber-protective of your gadgets, and may well be sick of shrieking 'don't touch the screen' as one of your kids moves perilously close to the computer with an extended chocolatey finger. Should the worst happen and you discover fingerprints all over the TV screen then at least you should be able to identify the culprit. Once identified, walk them through the following cleaning process and see how quickly they reoffend.

Conventional polish on glass, and particularly an LCD screen, is a complete no-no, so a solution of water and white vinegar in equal measures is best. Locate a lint-free cloth such as a microfibre towel, and apply a sprinkling of the cleaning solution onto the cloth. Turn off the appliance in question and, working around the screen in a gentle circular motion, remove the incriminating paw-prints.

If this rehabilitation programme does not work and they are found guilty of further offences then you are left with no other choice but to step up their punishment to car-cleaning level. Or make them wear gloves.

50. MAKE A MEMORY JAR

Inspired in part by Roald Dahl's concept of the 'Dream Jar' as demonstrated in *The BFG*, here we are using jars to create a physical diary of your family life over the years.

It's quite easy really: every time you go away, every special day or event that you enjoy as a family, remember to take an empty jar with you. Any type of transparent jar will do, and ideally never the same type of jar twice as you want to collect as many different shapes and sizes as possible over the years.

Once you have selected your jar then you and your team are ready to start collecting. Leaves, twigs, photos, receipts of significant meals, ticket stubs, bits of sheep wool, pebbles, score sheets from games played, doodles, photos, shells... Anything that might remind you of your experiences and adventures.

Once the holiday, event or whatever will constitute the memory to be recorded is over, then archive your pieces in the jar and shut the lid. Label it with the date, event and attendees, and then find an appropriate shelf to store your memories.

51. CHOOSE A SUITABLE PRINTER

Why do offices always have black-and-white printers? Because to print out emails, travel documents, invoices and spreadsheets in colour would be a complete waste of money, and a total drain on the world's resources. So why do we persist in buying colour printers for home use? Because we really do need that voucher for 30 per cent off at Gap to be in colour? I think not.

Next time you need to replace your printer, do the right thing and — for the same cost (or less) as a replacement colour cartridge or two — buy yourself a good old-fashioned black-and-white printer. And then enjoy the freedom of not wincing in pain as your child prints out some clipart — 'Go ahead, print out as many copies as you like,' you hear yourself say.

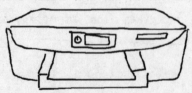

52. BEACHTIME FUN

MAKE DRINKING WATER FROM THIN AIR!

Imagine being washed up on a desert island with no source of fresh water. How will you survive? And then you remember many years ago your Dad taught you...

If it is a sunny and warm day, locate a piece of transparent plastic, ideally clingfilm — the largest you can find. Dig a hole in the damp sand about the diameter of the clingfilm and place an empty cup/vessel in the centre of the hole. Using pebbles to secure the clingfilm in place, cover the hole and then carefully place a light pebble on the film so that it creates a dimple just above, but not touching, the cup. Then watch and wait as the damp sand produces condensation, which collects on the underside of the clingfilm and drips into the cup. Voila! — drinking water.

53. CONFOUND AND ASTOUND WITH A CARD TRICK

Dynamo, David Blaine — step aside. Here comes Dad.

1) Welcome your audience and select your victim. Ask them to cut the pack and give it a good shuffle, then place the cards back on the table.

2) Instruct them to select the top card from the pack, memorise it, and place it back on the top.

3) In advance of your debut performance you would have perfected this one skill. Take the pack in your dominant hand, and then go to shuffle, but with the thumb of your non-dominant hand slide the top card from the top while depositing the rest of the cards above the top card. The top card will now be at the bottom of the pack.

4) In one slick move begin the shuffling action again while catching a glimpse of the bottom card, and also doing your best to disguise your hoopla.

5) Now you have the card in your mind's eye the rest is smoke and mirrors. Ask them to shuffle the pack themselves. Count out the cards into piles and pretend it is a counting trick. Make a mistake or two, but finally identify their original card.

Your ability to recreate this successfully time after time depends entirely on your ability to keep the method in your madness secret. Although it might be best to perform this only to minors — adults have a nasty habit of paying too much attention to what you are doing.

54. IMPROVISE A
BEDTIME STORY

Pick one from each category and let your
imagination do the rest.

HERO
YOUR KID'S NAME
(pretty much always)

HERO'S MAGIC POWER
FLIGHT
X-RAY VISION
MIDAS TOUCH
LIGHTNING SPEED
SUPER FART-POWER
TIME TRAVEL

SIDEKICK
SIBLING
PET CAT/DOG/BUDGIE
YOU
A DRAGON
BEST FRIEND
R2-D2

55. DAD DANCING WORKSHOP

Perfect your moves and
embarrass your kin to boot!

MORRISSEYESQUE

You know what to do! Untuck your shirt,
borrow someone's spectacles, grab the
flowers out of the vase (ideally gladioli),
and then begin to beat your rump with the
flora in time to the music while adopting
the expression of a cat urinating on an
antique rug. Keep going until all the petals
are gone along with anyone else on the
dance floor and what was left of your
self-respect. Now you have the DANCE FLOOR
to yourself you can properly create.

'There is a light that never goes out...'

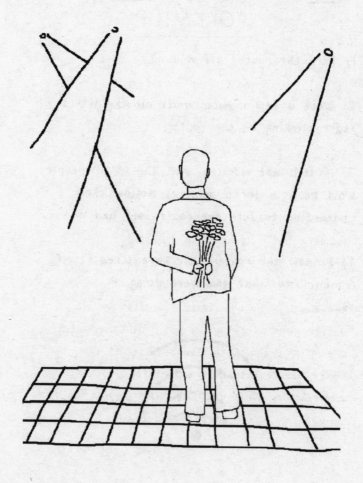

56. FIX THE WI-FI

1) Turn the router off and on.

2) Wait a few minutes until all the lights start blinking on the router.

3) If still not working, call the Wi-Fi people, wait on hold for 16 minutes, follow their instruction to turn the router off and on.

4) By now the router will have fixed itself. Go back to what you were doing.

57. MAKING SENSE
OF IT ALL...

'When my kids were younger, I used to avoid
them. I used to sit on the toilet 'til my legs
fell asleep. You want to know why your
father spends so long in the toilet? Because
he's not sure he wants to be a father.'

LOUIS C.K.

58. HOW TO MAKE A FREAKSHAKE

WARNING — If you and your kids don't know what a freakshake is then best to leave it this way.

If you and your kids do know what they are then you know that this is the DADDY of all treats, and should only be used in an emergency, or under extreme duress. With enough calories to last a week and a list of ingredients to make even the sweetest of teeth ache, this treat will put you in your kid's good books for weeks to come. Remind yourself of this as you scrape the chocolate syrup off the work surface, and watch out for mood-swings as your children crash and burn for a few hours after consumption. Good luck.

A recipe idea follows, but feel free to improvise. You basically need some ice cream and milk to make a milk shake (add fruit if your kids will let you), some whipped cream, a sticky syrupy substance, some sprinkles, and a cakey, biscuity thing for the top. Also, a large Mason jar or some kind of transparent drinking vessel, ideally with a handle.

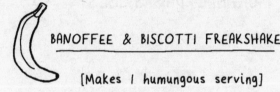

BANOFFEE & BISCOTTI FREAKSHAKE

[Makes 1 humungous serving]

INGREDIENTS

2 scoops of vanilla ice cream
1 glass of milk
1 banana — half frozen, half not
1 small tin of dulce de leche
1 glass of double cream
2 digestive biscuits, 1 whole and 1 in crumbs
Half a small bar of milk chocolate, grated

METHOD

Blend 1 scoop of ice cream, the half a frozen banana and the milk together and pour the milkshake into the Mason jar. Add in the final ice cream scoop and then decorate the uncovered inside and the rim of the jar with the dulce de leche. As carefully as you can, apply the digestive crumbs to the sticky dulce de leche on the inside and the rim. Whip the cream into soft peaks and, using a piping bag, pile the cream onto the shake so it erupts from the top of the jar. Sprinkle with grated chocolate and drizzle some more dulce de leche on top, then finish by balancing the remaining banana and digestive on the summit. Be creative, and for once it is OK to be messy.

59. MAKE DRAGON'S BLOOD FROM WATER (AND RED CABBAGE)

Put on your cloak and your best Professor Snape sneer and perform this most wizarding of experiments. Good for Halloween, birthday parties and christenings (actually, probably not christenings).

1) Fill a large jug with water and add about half a chopped red cabbage. Leave to soak for a few hours then strain out the leaves to reveal a purple liquid.

2) Share the base liquid among the assembled pupils — they will need two glasses' worth each.

3) Then provide each of the pupils with a small amount of white vinegar, and when you give the signal instruct them to pour the vinegar into the first glass. It will turn red, not quite the correct shade for human blood, but with a bit of dramatic licence you should be able to convince them.

4) To the final glass they will need to add a spoonful of washing powder, and this should reveal a green liquid — dragon's blood.

The science behind this may be fresher in the minds of your children from school chemistry lessons but, just to refresh you, red cabbage contains a natural pH indicator (anthocyanin). So when you add an acid (vinegar) it turns red, and when you add an alkali (washing powder) it turns green. If you have any of the liquid left, experiment with other everyday ingredients to see whether they are acid or alkali.

60. FIVE GREAT FAMILY MOVIES ON NETFLIX* YOU MIGHT NOT HAVE SEEN
(or not seen for a while)

*Presently on Netflix in the UK but are subject to change and differ from region to region.

Sunday afternoon, it's raining outside and it's family movie time. These recommendations should suit most tastes and you might even stay awake till the end!

1) *The Little Prince (2015)*
Antoine de Saint-Exupéry's classic story retold
for a new generation.

2) *Fantastic Mr. Fox (2009)*
Wes Anderson's idiosyncratic reworking of the
Roald Dahl favourite with a super-cool cast
of voices led by George Clooney and Meryl
Streep.

3) *Explorers (1985)*
A true 80s-style sci-fi fantasy blockbuster
starring a young Ethan Hawke and the
much-missed River Phoenix.

4) *The Curse of the Were-Rabbit (2005)*
More crazy adventures from Wallace and
Gromit as they battle a mutant rabbit.

5) *Into the Woods (2014)*
Who would have thought a Stephen Sondheim
musical would have made such an entertaining
family movie? See for yourself.

61. GO FOR A CHRISTMAS DAY SWIM IN THE OUTDOORS

This skill might seem like complete and utter madness in a winter climate, and is certainly not for everyone, but the benefits are strange and beautiful. It is every Dad's job to occasionally surprise, to do something unexpected and wonderful. OK — maybe this is overstating it, but it really will give your family a good laugh, and at the very least will cure any hangover you might have.

1) In advance of the big day, recruit some fellow nutters and arrange a time to meet at the local beach, pond, lake or outside swimming pool. Mid-morning is good.

2) Assuming swimming is safe, and adhering to a strict ban on wet suits, all participants must charge in unison towards the water.

3) What happens next often becomes the stuff of legend. Some whimper, some scream, some roar and some cry. But all are unified in the glory of what happens when Man defies the odds.

4) For the watchers it is a jolly good laugh, and time to pop a few Champagne corks. But for your kids, it may just hint at a surprising carefree side of yourself that once roamed free and dared to dream. Or not.

62. GET EVERYONE OUT THE DOOR IN THE MORNING ON SCHEDULE FOR A FAMILY EVENT

'This year we are not going to be late. This year we are not going to be late.' You repeat the mantra, but guess what, somehow, you are always late! Desperate times call for desperate measures.

Mission 1

In the dead of night on the eve of the event secure all distraction devices (phones, tablets, etc.) in the house and store securely in a secret location. This will speed up activity in the morning, and will aid your next step...

Mission 2

Estimate how late you normally are and, you guessed it, add that amount to every clock in the house. If you are lucky they might be dressed and out of the house before they cotton on.

63. MAKE A MUD PIE

You know you want to!

1) Get some wet mud.

2) Make it into a pie shape.

3) Don't eat it.

4) Do throw it around while doing your best impression of Daddy Pig.

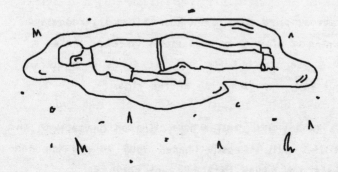

64. THE BREAKFAST OF CHAMPIONS

PANCAKES

This easy-peasy recipe will get everyone out of bed the moment the odour wafts up through the house, and makes about 10 'American' sized pancakes.

It is supplied with apologies to any US readers who may have their own views on what makes a good pancake, but for the rest of us is a quick and easy approximation of the classic.

It's also worth considering taking on an apprentice as this skill is easily handed down to any junior chefs old enough to handle hot pans!

1) In a mixing bowl measure out 2 good-sized mugs of self-raising flour, 2 mugs of milk and crack in 2 medium eggs. Add a pinch of salt and mix all together until you have a smooth paste-like consistency.

2) Then grate an apple or pear or any soft fruit you think might work — you are looking to add a bit of texture and sweetness — and mix in to the batter.

3) If you want to defy your stereotype and save time by multi-tasking then take two small frying pans and place over a medium heat, then add a knob of butter or some oil.

4) Into the pans ladle an equal amount of the batter. Once bubbles start to burst through on the surface it's time to make your big decision — do you flip or chicken out and reach for the utensils? Either way the pancakes are ready when golden brown on each side.

5) Keep warm in the oven and serve with maple syrup, Nutella, strawberries, blueberries, or just good old lemon and sugar.

65. 10 EMBARRASSING DAD JOKES WHILE CAMPING

1. Patient: Doctor, sometimes I feel like I'm a marquee, and sometimes I think I'm a wigwam.
   Doctor: Ah, your problem is you're two tents.

2. What happened to the lazy campers?
   They were charged with loitering within tent.

3. William Shakespeare opened a camping shop and put a sign in the window:
   'Now is the winter of our discount tent.'

4. Two men were out camping and started following some tracks. One man said they were deer tracks and the other man said they were badger tracks. They were still arguing when the train hit them.

5. Who drives round the West Country in a camper van?
   Tess of the Dormobiles.

6. Sherlock Holmes and Dr Watson were camping. Holmes woke Watson in the middle of the night and asked him: 'Look at the sky, Watson, and tell me what you can deduce.'
'It appears to be a clear night. Why, what do you deduce, Holmes?'
'Watson, you idiot, someone has stolen our tent!'

7. Why did the native American wear a fur hat?
To keep his wigwam.

8. What happened to the stupid sea scout?
His tent sank.

9. Policeman: Excuse me, sir, I've pulled you over because I noticed you have a defective rear light.
Motorist: Oh no, that's awful, what on earth am I going to do?
Policeman: Don't worry, sir, it's not that serious.
Motorist: It flippin' well is — where's my caravan gone?!

10. Two Aussies were camping in the wilderness when one was bitten on the bum by a deadly snake. His mate phoned the Flying Doctor who told him unless the poison was sucked out quickly his friend would die. The wounded camper asked, 'What did the doc say, mate?'
'He says you're going to die, mate.'

66. COLLECT THE DADDY TAX

'Any child upon this earth, in receipt of cakes, sweets, crisps or any foodstuff that the father liketh, shall give up a tithe of no less than 1 in 10 parts of the whole. Failure to pay the tithe will result in confiscation of the aforementioned foodstuff.'

Extract from the *Tibetan Book of the Dad.*

If your children don't believe in this ancient law then show them the proof above, and happily help yourself to your rightful share. And if they still don't believe it then point out that this is a valuable lesson in economics, and when they eventually do pay tax they won't just be paying 10 per cent.

This skill also relates to the other important duty that a parent must perform — official food-taster. Sometimes you need more than one bite to confirm the food is not poisoned...

67. HONEY AND LEMON COUGH TREATMENT

There is some evidence that honey and lemon might help with the symptoms of a cold, such as a sore throat, and although it is probably only a placebo, that is often a very effective remedy in treating a sick child. Therefore:

1) Mix 2 teaspoons of honey with a good squeeze of fresh lemon juice and add hot water to taste.

2) When at a suitable drinking temperature, serve to the child.

3) You may want to combine this treatment with an over-the-counter children's paracetamol or ibuprofen-based oral suspension fluid. Always follow the manufacturers' dosage instructions.

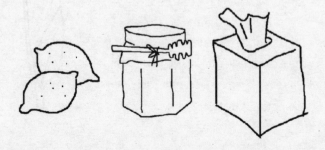

68. ATTRACT BUTTERFLIES AND BEES TO YOUR GARDEN

If you have a garden, chances are you have a patch of ground that you really don't know what to do with? Maybe there is a pile of flowerpots there, or it is a lost kingdom down the side of the trampoline? Whatever — now is the time to put this fallow ground to good use and build a living, breathing home for bees and butterflies.

1) Enlist the help of an accomplice, head off to the garden centre and purchase a wildflower seed-bomb, or just some seeds.

2) Locate the area you wish to transform and clear away any stray weeds and grass that will interfere with your plans. Make sure there is reasonable drainage and sufficient sunlight. If nothing is presently growing there then perhaps best to find another spot.

3) Following the planting instructions, sow the seeds. Or just do the typical Dad thing: scatter randomly and see what nature brings.

If you don't have a garden, or even if you do, it can be fun to repeat the above plan on a piece of public land that needs brightening up, and then return back year after year to enjoy your gift to Mother Nature.

69. KITCHEN PLAYLIST

If it's a baking day or they're tackling some kitchen-based homework task, then keep you and the kids interested with a custom-made bespoke soundtrack to your activities.

Create your own or try this one for size:

Side A	Side B
• 'Soul Kitchen' — The Doors	• 'Kitchen' — The Lemonheads
• 'Food Glorious Food' (from Oliver!) — Original cast recording	• 'Stir It Up' — Bob Marley & the Wailers
• 'Rat in Mi Kitchen' — UB40	• 'Martika's Kitchen' — Martika
• 'Kitchen Table' — Jake Bugg	• 'Savoy Truffle' — The Beatles
• 'Hey, Good Lookin'' — Hank Williams	• 'You'll Always Find Me in the Kitchen at Parties' — Jona Lewie
• 'Coconut' — Harry Nilsson	• 'Roast Fish & Cornbread' — Lee 'Scratch' Perry

70. KEEP THE GUTTERS CLEAR

'Hooray — gutters and drainpipes!' you exclaim. This may be one of those chores that you remember your Dad doing and thinking, 'What a sad man.' And here you are 30-odd years later contemplating the same conclusion about yourself as a river of water cascades down the side of your house rather than along the gutter and down the drainpipes.

Leaves, crisp packets, twigs and bits of tile all conspire to cause the blockage, and if you don't take action you may find your property becomes a rather oversized water feature in your garden. If you don't want to risk life and limb scooping it all out each year, perched perilously atop a super-long ladder, then:

1) Borrow a super-long ladder. Or better still enlist the window cleaner.

2) Purchase a suitable length of gutter brush or hedgehog guard. This is like a long bottle brush that is secured in the gutter and fills the space, preventing debris from settling.

3) Clear the gutters for one last time (hopefully) and secure the gutter brush, or get your hired hand to do it for you.

71. HOW TO MAKE PAPER LOOK OLD

Whether it's pirate treasure maps, history homework, themed party invitations or just general imaginative craft play, this is a very handy skill to teach to your kids. You are aiming for that weather-beaten leathery look that you might find used in a *Pirates of the Caribbean* movie — and I'm talking about a paper prop and not Keith Richards' face!

1) Either print (selecting an 'Olde Worlde' font) or hand-write your text on regular paper, whatever size suits your needs.

2) Screw up the paper into a ball and then unfold.

3) Either make or recycle some old cold coffee or tea (coffee will produce a darker-tinted paper).

4) Place the paper into a shallow baking dish and then pour the liquid over the paper, making sure it is exposed to the fluid on both sides.

5) Gently rub the paper around the edges with your fingers until you feel it starting to erode.

6) Leave for an hour or two and then carefully pour away the liquid, making sure that the paper does not break. Gently remove the paper and place on a tea towel to dry.

72. BEACHTIME FUN

SCAVENGE FOR FLOTSAM AND JETSAM

Scavenging was once a full-time occupation, and can be rewarding not only in the sense of what you find, but also via the benefits gained from wandering aimlessly for an hour or two with your loved ones. If you didn't already know it, FLOTSAM is defined as debris accidentally lost from a vessel and JETSAM is defined as debris deliberately thrown overboard. Collect it and sort into piles of what you imagine to be flotsam and jetsam and then create a story as to how the object found its way there? Pirate ship? Warship? Drunken tourist?

And if you have a metal detector then you can up the ante and go full-on treasure hunting.

73. OWN THE CALENDAR

If you don't presently maintain the family calendar then perhaps it is time for you to take a turn. Just the fact that you know when things are happening will mean you are more responsible and, in turn, more involved with the events that matter to your kids. If you can't be at home all the time, then at least be aware of what is going on when you are not there, and plan the best use of your time for when you are there.

A physical calendar is still pretty much the only way to do it, although app developers will try to persuade you otherwise. If you can, allocate space for each family member for each day, and it is a good thing to try to teach them to add in their own events. And a yearly personalised photo calendar is another good idea as you can store any recurring dates there (it's also a good excuse to go through all the family photos).

74. CAST A SPELL AROUND THE HOUSE AT HALLOWEEN

This is a traditional skill that pre-dates the modern trend of trick or treating, and in certain parts of Essex has been handed down through the generations for centuries. It involves a little bit of preparation and a whole heap of Vincent Price / Christopher Lee* style horror camp, although you don't want to cause nightmares so take it easy on the bloodcurdling screams.

1) Once night has fallen, and before everyone heads off trick or treating, gather the family at the threshold of your house / apartment / castle.

2) Utilising all the lanterns and torches you can muster from around the house, hand them out and illuminate.

3) Now begins the incantation that will protect you and yours from evil spirits all year round. Repeat in a sombre tone the spell on the next page as you go.

*delete as appropriate.

4) As Head Wizard you will lead the procession, which should progress sedately and circle each room in the property, before heading out to the garden and outbuildings, and then circling back through the front door.

5) The house is now secure from evil spirits for a further year, but don't forget to repeat the spell every Halloween, or who knows what misfortune will befall you...

FRIENDLY SPIRITS ALL AROUND US,

KEEP US SAFE FOR ALL THIS YEAR.

DO NOT LET THE WITCH
CONFOUND US,

PROTECT US, WE THAT
GATHER HERE.

75. SAY GOODBYE TO A DEAD PET

The trauma of a pet's death is a very good way to begin to introduce this life lesson to your children, so the way you design your final goodbye to your pet can be very educational as well as comforting.

How to grieve is a very personal choice we make, and you most certainly will have your own ideas on the best way to approach this with your loved ones. What follows are just a few ideas to get you thinking.

- Many pets will end their days in the vet's surgery, and whether to bring your children to witness their final moments may be one of the biggest decisions you will make together. Talk it through and they will make their choice with your support.

- It is perfectly OK in the UK to bury your pets in the garden as long as they are not considered a health hazard and you own the land. Make sure you dig a hole deep enough to ensure you don't tempt any furry gravediggers.

- Hold a wake and invite the family to contribute poems, letters and songs. Slightly tongue in cheek (maybe suitable for a goldfish?), you might want to dress all in black and play sombre music as you read your elegies. You could even construct a mini-coffin and lower it, and then follow up with a scattering of earth and a mini-bouquet of daisies? Or play it straight.

76. DAD DANCING WORKSHOP

Perfect your moves and
embarrass your kin to boot!

THE LIMBO

A staple of the post-BBQ entertainment, but
not to be attempted without a full crew
of medics on hand to attend to a slipped
disc, or to extract a BBQ skewer from
somewhere it shouldn't be. As it is a BBQ
you will of course already be wearing a
Hawaiian shirt and flower garland, so you
are halfway there.

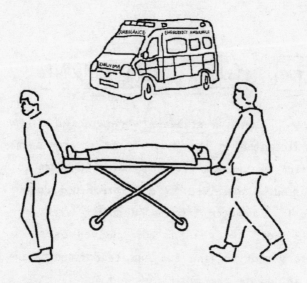

To style yourself further, grab the last meat-laden skewer that is now finally cooked but cold, and place between your teeth. In one hand hold a cocktail, and (if available) in the other some maracas. A quick shuffle of the shoulders and then begin your descent...

77. GET THEM CODING

Over 100 million students worldwide have now participated in the 'Hour of Code' programme, hosted on the non-profit website CODE.org. Originally conceived as a tutorial aid during the US Computer Science Education Week in 2013, Hour of Code has now evolved as a free portal to find fun and educational ways to introduce the basics of coding.

Endorsed by the likes of Barack Obama and Bill Gates, Hour of Code is used in schools and homes all over the world, and features non-profit introductions from children's favourites such as Minecraft, Star Wars and Gumball. If you would like to give your kids a taster, head to the Hourofcode.com website and click on the How-to Parents link.

78. MAKING SENSE OF IT ALL...

'I believe that what we become depends on what our fathers teach us at odd moments, when they aren't trying to teach us. We are formed by little scraps of wisdom.'

UMBERTO ECO

79. MAKE McSMORES

A relatively new introduction in other parts
of the world, the S'more has been popular
around campfires in the USA since the 1920s.
Traditionally it consists of a campfire-
toasted marshmallow and a layer of chocolate
sandwiched between two pieces of Graham
cracker (a Graham cracker is a wheat-based
biscuit, not unlike the British teatime
favourite, the digestive).

So what is a McSmore, you demand? The McSmore is the son of the S'more, and some might argue the pupil has become the master. Here we utilise the serendipity of the chocolate digestive biscuit. Take your golden-toasted, melting marshmallow and squish it Wagon Wheel-esque betwixt the chocolate sides of two biscuits. Voila — the perfect campfire treat.

But why McSmore? Because 'Mc' means 'son of' in Gaelic and the digestive is one of Scotland's greatest inventions.

80. THE BREAKFAST OF CHAMPIONS

FRENCH TOAST

Debate rages as to the origin of the term
French toast — does it derive from the French
term 'pain perdu' for 'lost bread' (stale bread
reclaimed) or was it named after the
17th-century New York innkeeper Joseph French?
Who knows, and for that matter who cares,
but one thing we all agree on is that French
toast is truly scrumdiddlyumptious.

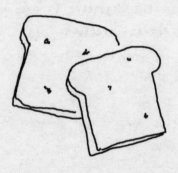

1) Crack one medium egg per two pieces of toast you plan to make into a large mixing bowl, add a large splash of milk, a few drops of vanilla essence and a teaspoon of white caster sugar. Hand whisk until you have a glossy liquid.

2) Heat the largest frying pan you have on a medium-low heat and add a knob of butter to coat the pan.

3) Take a slice of bread — thickly sliced white tends to work best — and dip into the batter for a few seconds on each side. Drip off the excess mix and put the bread in the pan. Repeat until you can't fit any more slices in.

4) Cook until the underside is starting to go a golden brown, and then flip with a spatula and cook the other side.

5) Sift a little icing sugar on top and serve with bacon, fruit, maple syrup...

81. RECITE A SHAKESPEARE MONOLOGUE

Is there anything more rousing than a fully grown man standing in a field belting out their own interpretation of one of the Bard's greatest monologues? Admittedly he may be dressed for camping and have had one beer too many, but there is glory to be found in any attempt to aspire to the heights of Olivier or Branagh.

If you are able to master at least some of the famous monologue on the next page then it may serve you well as spirits wane in the queue for the ferry, or stranded by the motorway waiting for roadside assistance. And you might find that you inspire a budding Dench or Rylance?

FROM HENRY V
(spoken by King Henry).

Once more unto the breach, dear friends, once more,
Or close the wall up with our English dead.
In peace there's nothing so becomes a man
As modest stillness and humility;
But when the blast of war blows in our ears,
Then imitate the action of the tiger:
Stiffen the sinews, conjure up the blood,
Disguise fair nature with hard-favoured rage.
Then lend the eye a terrible aspect;
Let pry through the portage of the head
Like the brass cannon; let the brow o'erwhelm it
As fearfully as doth a galled rock
O'erhang and jutty his confounded base,
Swilled with the wild and wasteful ocean.
Now set the teeth and stretch the nostril wide,
Hold hard the breath and bend up every spirit
To his full height. On, on, you noblest English,
Whose blood is fet from fathers of war-proof,
Fathers that, like so many Alexanders
Have in these parts from morn till even fought,
And sheathed their swords for lack of argument.
Dishonour not your mothers; now attest
That those whom you call'd fathers did beget you.
Be copy now to men of grosser blood
And teach them how to war. And you, good yeoman,
Whose limbs were made in England, show us here
The mettle of your pasture; let us swear
That you are worth your breeding which I doubt not,
For there is none of you so mean and base
That hath not noble lustre in your eyes.
I see you stand like greyhounds in the slips,
Straining upon the start. The game's afoot.
Follow your spirit, and upon this charge
Cry 'God for Harry, England, and Saint George!'

82. STICKY TOFFEE — THE ORIGINAL AND STILL THE BEST RUNNING-AROUND GAME

Depending on how many people you have playing, you will need about five runners per catcher. Each of the catchers needs to stand with their arms outstretched, and each runner grabs a finger. The lead catcher begins the game with the statement:

> 'I WENT TO THE SHOPS AND
> I BOUGHT SOME STICKY...'

Then they say anything beginning with the letter 't': it could be 'tomatoes', it could be 'tofu' or it could be 'tarantulas'. The catcher repeats the phrase until finally they bought some sticky TOFFEE!

At this point the runners run, and the catchers must tag. When a runner is tagged they must stand still and can only be set free by a fellow runner crawling under their legs. The game is over when all the runners are tagged, or everyone is exhausted.

83. <u>LEARN TO RELAX</u>

It is important to learn to relax — this will make you a better Dad. Therefore pamper yourself with the following and convince your children that this is all about providing a better service.

Choose 1 from each option:

Option 1
- PIZZA - CURRY - SLOW-COOKED LAMB SHANKS
- FISH AND CHIPS - BURRITO - ROAST CHICKEN
- BEEF BOURGUIGNON - SAUSAGES AND MASH

Option 2
- ICE CREAM - CHOCOLATE FUDGE CAKE - APPLE
PIE - RASPBERRY PANNA COTTA - FRUIT TRIFLE
- TIRAMISU - CHEESE SELECTION - BANOFFEE PIE

Option 3
- CZECH LAGER - LARGE RIOJA - FLAT WHITE
- INDIA PALE ALE - CHENIN BLANC - G&T
- DOUBLE ESPRESSO - BOURBON - SCOTCH

Now repeat option 3 until totally relaxed.

84. BREAKFAST OF CHAMPIONS

SOUS VIDE AN EGG IN A PAN

This is a journey that you might want to bring some of the more scientific-minded members of your household on with you? If you have any budding Heston Blumenthals or Marie Curies then wake them up a few minutes early, don your goggles and white coats and fire up the Bunsen burners.

From the French for 'under vacuum', sous vide is typified by a style of cooking where food is vacuum-packed in plastic and then slow-poached in a water bath at an exact temperature. Limited in its ability to brown foods, it has the benefit of being able to cook food, particularly meat, to an exact temperature while retaining all its juices and flavour.

Chefs have been using sous vide baths for decades now, but up until recently they were too expensive for your average geeky Dad. It is now possible to buy a reasonably priced sous vide water bath for the domestic kitchen, but before you rush out and add to the collection of forgotten gadgets stashed somewhere in your kitchen, why not try this experiment using conventional kitchen tools?

THE OBJECTIVE

To make the perfect soft-boiled/poached egg with a thick and luscious yolk that is silky smooth.

THE METHOD

In the case of an egg, Mother Nature has conveniently vacuum-packed its bounty already, so no need for plastic bags and a vacuum-sealing machine. One crucial piece of kit you will need though is a digital thermometer, and using this you will need to regulate the heat of a large pan of water at 70C / 158F. This might take a bit of tinkering, but you need to find the best way possible to maintain that temperature.

Your egg should be as fresh as possible, and the times given below for this experiment are calibrated for what European supermarkets might call a 'large' egg (in the US it would be a size 'extra large') or about 65g. Like all good scientists, make sure you weigh your egg to record as much data as possible to aid your quest for perfection. The egg must also be at room temperature.

Plunge the egg into the home-made sous vide machine and keep a constant eye on the temperature as the egg cooks. After 21 minutes exactly extract the egg and begin the dissection, with either toast or muffins.

85. 10 EMBARRASSING DAD JOKES FOR IN THE CAR

1. What's big, red and lies upside-down in the gutter?
   A dead bus.

2. I bet my friend I could make a car out of macaroni... You should have seen her face when I drove pasta.

3. What do you call a man with a car on his head?
   Jack.

4. Why did the man with no alarm clock sleep under his old banger?
   He wanted to wake up oily in the morning.

5. Doctor: You appear to have a steering wheel attached to your groin.
   Man: Yes, and it's driving me nuts!

6. Why didn't the chicken cross the road?
   He saw what happened to the zebra.

7. How did the car get a puncture?
   From the fork in the road!

8. What happened to the man who lived in
   a car tyre?
   He had a puncture, and now he lives in
   a flat.

9. What do you call a vicar on a motorbike?
   Rev.

10. What happened to the frog who stopped
    on a double-yellow line?
    He was toad away.

86. ORGANISE A HARRY POTTER BIRTHDAY PARTY

In all probability your kids will at some point become obsessed with Harry Potter — the books, the movies or both. When your child sees a chopstick, grabs it and immediately yells, 'EXPELLIARMUS!' then you know that time has arrived.

If you have the time and are prepared to make a fool of yourself (again) then this can be quite an economical birthday party to arrange. However, if you follow through with the role-playing then prepare to be attacked for weeks to come by budding Harrys and Hermiones at school pick-up.

1) Make your own invitations. Go to skill $\boxed{71}$ to see how to make parchment-looking paper. Print or handwrite and then inscribe 'sent by owl' on the envelope.

2) First costume change — The Fat Lady. Dress appropriately and greet each attendee at the threshold demanding the pre-arranged password for entry.

3) The Sorting Hat. If you are able, rig up a bluetooth speaker so you can talk from another room, then assign each kid a house (perhaps don't bother with Hufflepuff, Ravenclaw and Slytherin — they'll all want to be in Gryffindor).

4) Second costume change — Professor Snape. Take a potions class — see skill $\boxed{59}$ for suitable and safe science-based potions.

5) Make Butterbeer. See skill $\boxed{10}$.

6) Third costume change — Voldemort. Stage the final battle with you cast as He Who Must Not Be Named. Pre-make a batch of water bombs, grab as many super-soakers and water pistols as you can and head outside. Prepare your best snarling voice and expect a soaking.

7) Send every kid home with a Honeydukes branded party bag, and a home-made wand (see skill $\boxed{93}$) from Ollivanders.

87. GET RID OF NITS AND HEADLICE

As soon as your children start getting out there and moving among the great unwashed there is a very good chance that one day you will find them obsessively scratching their head. There are two solutions to this problem that don't use chemicals and absolutely do work. One is called the Nitty Gritty Nit Comb, and once you discover it you may find yourself logging on to Amazon and writing gushing 5-star reviews. The other is to shave your child's head — Kojak bald.

Assuming you choose the former method rather than the latter then see below.

1) There are other nit combs out there, but the Nitty Gritty really does work (and no, I don't have any affiliation with this company).

2) At bathtime, wet the infected patient's head and apply hair conditioner liberally.

3) Then comb into sections so you can be sure that you methodically cover all of the head.

4) Now the fun bit. As you comb you will notice lice and little white eggs (which may be invisible in the conditioner) coming away with the excess conditioner. Wipe this onto a towel, and keep combing until you have covered the whole head.

5) Repeat this process every few days for as long as it takes.

88. MOTIVATIONAL CHORES PLAYLIST

Before your children begin to develop their own musical taste it is every father's duty to attempt to imprint his own musical preferences upon his kin. With that in mind, create a playlist that you can use as a soundtrack to help ease them through the turmoil of tidying their room, washing the car or mowing the lawn. Or just use it to try and get them off the sofa!

See the next page for one I made earlier:

Side A	Side B
- 'Cherry Bomb' (from Guardians of the Galaxy) — The Runaways	- 'Get Up Offa That Thing' — James Brown
- 'Whistle While You Work' (from Snow White) — Adriana Caselotti	- 'Firestarter' — The Prodigy
- 'Walk This Way' — Run DMC, Aerosmith	- 'Crazy in Love' — Beyonce
- 'Respect' — Aretha Franklin	- 'Get Up, Stand Up' — Bob Marley & the Wailers
- 'Twist and Shout' — The Beatles	- 'Do It' — The Pink Fairies
	- 'Working in the Coal Mine' — Lee Dorsey

89. MEND A BIKE PUNCTURE

The most time-efficient way to deal with this problem would be to keep a stock of replacement inner tubes, but certainly the most cost-efficient solution is to use a bicycle puncture repair kit.

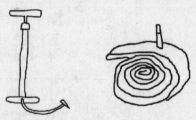

1) Once you have taken the wheel off the bike make sure you let out all the remaining air in the tyre before you start work. Insert a tyre lever (or the handle of a dessert spoon) under the rim of the tyre by the valve and hoick it over the rim of the wheel so the lever is held in place. Next take the other tyre lever and insert it between the tyre and the wheel next to the first lever, then carefully run the lever along the circumference of the wheel rim away from the first lever. The tyre should come away from the wheel. Repeat on the other side.

2) Take the inner tube and tyre away from the wheel but before you take the inner tube away from the tyre, mark on the tyre with chalk where the valve is and then put the inner tube to one side. Starting at the chalk mark, run your fingers around the inside of the tyre feeling for the cause of the puncture. Hopefully you will find something that has penetrated — remove this carefully. The puncture in the inner tube should be found roughly the same distance from the valve as the distance from chalk mark to hole in the tyre.

3) If you cannot find the puncture on the inner tube (or the hole in the tyre), plan B is to re-inflate the tube and listen for a hiss. Plan C — submerge in a bucket of water and squeeze, looking for air bubbles.

4) Now you have located the puncture, mark it with the chalk and, using the sandpaper supplied in the kit, gently rub the area around the hole to make it rough and more amenable to adhesion.

5) Finally, apply the sticky patch, taking care not to touch the sticky side, and leave until you are confident it is stuck firmly. Test the inner tube and put everything back together again.

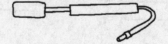

90. MAKE A LEGO TABLE

The word 'make' here may be a little misleading. What we are doing is purchasing some Lego baseplates and sticking them to the top of a suitable desk or table in the lucky kid's bedroom. It's good to use a desk with a drawer, so you have a convenient storage space for the Lego pieces.

1) Source as many baseplates as you need to cover the area you want to fill. They are expensive, but very cheap compared to a proper custom-built Lego table.

2) Using some superglue or similar adhesive, stick the baseplates to the surface and leave to dry, weighted down, for 24 hours.

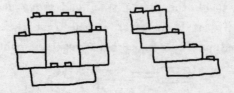

91. DO THE BIRDS AND THE BEES TALK

If you are taking responsibility for this one then the trick is just to do it. Don't dither. Sit your subject down and explain in as frank and caring a manner as possible.

Chances are they will just say 'yuck' and exit stage left. Oh — and whatever you do, don't let them Google it.

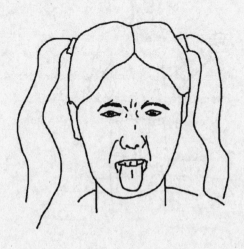

92. THE QUEST FOR THE STONE

'Ancient legends have told of THE STONE, so perfect in its evolution that it was as spherical as the sun. And when THE STONE is united with the one true finder, then peace will reign over the world.'

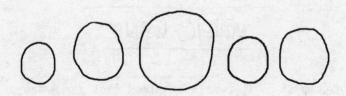

From the *Tibetan Book of the Dad*.

Put simply, your aim is to find the most spherical stone you can, and keep it in your pocket. When you find a better one, return the original to its source and pocket the superior one. Repeat your quest whenever you can.

To be used as a vehicle to spice up walks, this might fire your kids' imaginations or at the least provide an excuse to have a good old chat while you ramble across the countryside or stroll along the beach.

93. HOW TO MAKE A MAGIC WAND

DISCLAIMER — It isn't guaranteed that the wand will actually be magic but if you keep trying then you never know!

Magic wands are very useful these days — tidying bedrooms, putting up that shelf, running the kids to drama club. We can dream...

To make your kids their very own wand that would make Merlin proud then HEY PRESTO!

1) Visit the local garden centre, or nab from your neighbour's tomato plants a few bamboo canes.

2) Examine each cane and look for good wand-like pieces to cut to size, around 30cm (12 inches), something like that. As all good Wizards know, each wand is individual, so cut pieces that have character.

3) Now to finally utilise all those tins of paint testers that you couldn't bring yourself to throw away. Decorate each wand with stripes, spots, stars, glitter, gemstones, etc. Anything that adds a bit of pizazz. Or just varnish for an industrial utilitarian Wizard look?

4) Once fully dry, present to your child, inventing a suitable back-story, name, provenance etc. If you have time using skill 71 you could create a certificate of authenticity on faux aged paper.

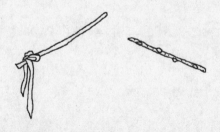

94. TOP DAD CLICHÉS

What goes around comes around. Not too long ago you were on the receiving end of these jibes, and you would groan and think, 'If I have kids they will be able to do what they want.' Fatherhood is a great leveller.

Examine the list below and try to avoid using these time-honoured phrases.

In no particular order:

- WERE YOU BORN IN A BARN? THEN CLOSE THE DOOR!

- TURN THE LIGHT OFF WHEN YOU LEAVE A ROOM!

- GIVE ME THE REMOTE CONTROL!

- BE QUIET — IT SOUNDS LIKE A HERD OF ELEPHANTS IN HERE!

- FINISH YOUR PLATE, THERE ARE PEOPLE STARVING IN AFRICA!

- ASK YOUR MUM!

- DO YOU THINK MONEY GROWS ON TREES?

- FEET OFF THE TABLE!

- DID YOU FLUSH THE TOILET?

- HAVE YOU BRUSHED YOUR TEETH?

- DID YOU PUT THE LID BACK ON THE
  TOOTHPASTE?

- YOU TREAT THIS PLACE LIKE A HOTEL!

- WHAT TIME DO YOU CALL THIS?!

- I AM NOT A CHAUFFEUR!

- WHAT DID YOUR LAST SLAVE DIE OF?

- WHEN I WAS A BOY/LAD...

- I REMEMBER WHEN ALL THIS WAS HILLS AND
  MEADOWS!

- I REALLY THINK YOU ARE GOING TO LIKE DARK
  SIDE OF THE MOON / OK COMPUTER /
  SCREAMADELICA (delete as appropriate)

95. DAD DANCING WORKSHOP

Perfect your moves and
embarrass your kin to boot!

BREAKDANCE!

Dust down your Caterpillar, calibrate your
Windmill and oil and service your Headspin
— let's BREAKDANCE! To achieve the full
effect of this it is best to lull the
audience into a false sense of security.
Encourage your kids onto the dance floor
with the most inoffensive moves you can
muster, something smoochy or just a gentle
side-step. You want them to feel like they
should be helping you out a bit.

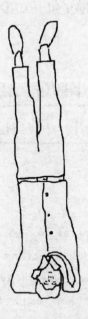

Once you have them on the dance floor, wait
for a tempo change and let it go. As you
moonwalk around them, chopping your hands at
their head and neck, they will realise all too
late that they are now contesting the most
radical of burns! As they step away awestruck
and dumbfounded it's time to unleash the
Headspin. Warning — those of us now follicly
challenged may need to double-layer our heads
for protection.

96. MAKING SENSE OF IT ALL...

'When I was a boy of 14, my father was so ignorant, I could hardly stand to have the old man around. But when I got to be 21, I was astonished at how much the old man had learned in seven years.'

MARK TWAIN

DE-ODOURISE THE KITCHEN

When the kitchen sink drain is causing a smell that might normally be attributed to Uncle ****** (insert name here) then you know it is time to take action.

This solution is cheap and does not use any chemicals that are harmful to the environment.

1) Pour one mug of baking soda down the plug hole, followed by two mugs of boiling water.

2) Wait a few minutes while the baking soda does its job and begins to break down the muck that has solidified there.

3) Next, mix together a mug of boiling water and a mug of white vinegar, and pour down the plughole.

4) Plug the hole and listen for the mini-eruption as the vinegar reacts to the baking soda and clears the yucky muck.

5) When the controlled explosion is over pour down some more boiling water and tick that 'job done' box.

98. LIVING WITH SNAPCHAT

Do you remember letters? Pen-pals? Faxes?
If so you might struggle slightly in coming
to terms with some modern communication
techniques but, like all innovations, it pays
to approach them with an open mind.
Regardless of your views, your children will
probably already be down with it before you
have had your input anyway.

By the end of 2016 Snapchat had over 156
million users worldwide and is commonly
referred to as the media choice of the
'millennials'. In utilising the ability to send
a photo or video which, once viewed, is
deleted after the sender's designated viewing
time has elapsed, the sender retains privacy
as the media can't be passed on or shared.

Another popular feature of Snapchat is the ability to add 'filters', which add a layer of animation to a selfie photo or video. So if you ever wondered what you looked like with bunny ears and a cute bunny nose, then wonder no more!

Is Snapchat safe for your child? That is a decision for you to make with them.

99. TREAT A BEE STING

Is it luckier to have been stung by a bee rather than a wasp? Certainly luckier for the stinger to be a wasp as, unlike the bee, it will live to sting another day. If your child has been stung they probably won't care what insect was their assailant, but you will need to know, as a bee infamously leaves its sting imbedded intact in the skin.

1) Using a credit card, scrape the stinger away from the site, and do not pinch the skin. The longer you leave the stinger in, the more venom is released, and the more pain your child will endure.

2) Apply some kind of pain relief to the sting site if you are able, either a sting cream or there are a whole host of natural remedies such as ice (sensible), toothpaste (messy) and raw onion (stinky). You choose.

3) Check for symptoms of any allergic reaction, and if you notice anything out of the ordinary then seek immediate medical advice.

100. FIVE FAMILY MOVIES ON AMAZON PRIME* YOU MIGHT NOT HAVE SEEN

(or not seen for a while)

These five are suitable for that special family movie moment. No devices allowed, and that includes you too!

1) *Song of the Sea* (2014)
Oscar-nominated, this hand-drawn animated movie
has its roots in Celtic folklore, and tells a
funny, heart-warming tale of family life.

2) *The Lego Movie* (2014)
Seen it already one hundred times? Then once
more won't hurt — and if you haven't seen it
then everything will be awesome.

3) *Paddington* (2014)
Live action reworking of Michael Bond's
books that cleverly works for a modern
multi-generational audience.

4) *The Lorax* (2012)
Danny DeVito leads a voice-cast including
Zac Efron and Taylor Swift; adapted from
Dr. Seuss's 1971 classic book.

5) *Bill* (2015)
From the team behind the BBC's *Horrible Histories*,
this is the imagined story of William Shakespeare's
rise from obscurity to immortal bard.

*Presently on Amazon Prime in the UK but are
subject to change and differ from region to region.

101.

I ♥ YOU

Don't forget to tell them
how much you love them.

THIS VOUCHER IS PRESENTED TO THE

BEST DAD

IN THE WORLD IN RECOGNITION OF

EXCELLENCE IN THE FIELD OF PARENTING

AND ENTITLES THE BEARER TO...

Breakfast in bed.

AMAZING

VOUCHER

THIS VOUCHER IS PRESENTED TO THE

BEST DAD

IN THE WORLD IN RECOGNITION OF

EXCELLENCE IN THE FIELD OF PARENTING

AND ENTITLES THE BEARER TO....

A home-made cake of their choice.

AMAZING

DAD

VOUCHER

THIS VOUCHER IS PRESENTED TO THE

BEST DAD

IN THE WORLD IN RECOGNITION OF

EXCELLENCE IN THE FIELD OF PARENTING

AND ENTITLES THE BEARER TO...

One free carwash and valet.

AMAZING

**DAD**

VOUCHER

THIS VOUCHER IS PRESENTED TO THE

BEST DAD

IN THE WORLD IN RECOGNITION OF

EXCELLENCE IN THE FIELD OF PARENTING

AND ENTITLES THE BEARER TO...

A two-hour shed / garden / DIY slot.

AMAZING

VOUCHER

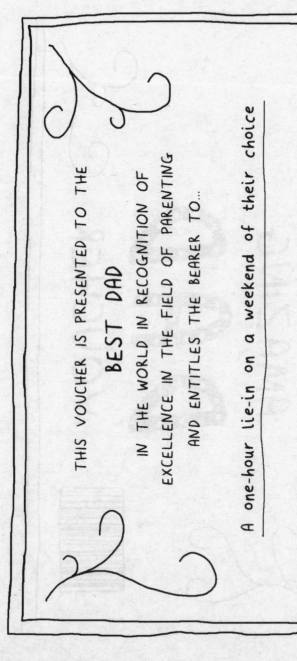

THIS VOUCHER IS PRESENTED TO THE

BEST DAD

IN THE WORLD IN RECOGNITION OF
EXCELLENCE IN THE FIELD OF PARENTING
AND ENTITLES THE BEARER TO...

A one-hour lie-in on a weekend of their choice

AMAZING
DAD

VOUCHER

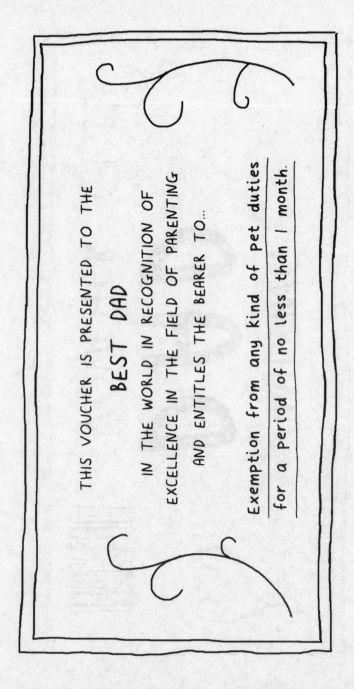

THIS VOUCHER IS PRESENTED TO THE

BEST DAD

IN THE WORLD IN RECOGNITION OF

EXCELLENCE IN THE FIELD OF PARENTING

AND ENTITLES THE BEARER TO...

Exemption from any kind of pet duties

for a period of no less than 1 month.

AMAZING  VOUCHER

THIS VOUCHER IS PRESENTED TO THE

BEST DAD

IN THE WORLD IN RECOGNITION OF

EXCELLENCE IN THE FIELD OF PARENTING

AND ENTITLES THE BEARER TO...

A half-hour (forty winks)

mid-afternoon snooze.

AMAZING

VOUCHER

THIS VOUCHER IS PRESENTED TO THE

BEST DAD

IN THE WORLD IN RECOGNITION OF
EXCELLENCE IN THE FIELD OF PARENTING
AND ENTITLES THE BEARER TO...

A guaranteed tidy room for a
minimum of four weeks.

AMAZING

VOUCHER

THIS VOUCHER IS PRESENTED TO THE

BEST DAD

IN THE WORLD IN RECOGNITION OF
EXCELLENCE IN THE FIELD OF PARENTING
AND ENTITLES THE BEARER TO...

A minimum of one hour's tablet /
phone / TV time without interruption

AMAZING

DAD

VOUCHER

THIS VOUCHER IS PRESENTED TO THE

BEST DAD

IN THE WORLD IN RECOGNITION OF
EXCELLENCE IN THE FIELD OF PARENTING
AND ENTITLES THE BEARER TO....

A period of no less than 24 hours where
no child is allowed to use the word no.

AMAZING

DAD

VOUCHER